CUBAN *Exile*

A YOUNG GIRL'S JOURNEY

MIRIAM ISIDRO

Copyright © 2017 Miriam Isidro.

All rights reserved. No part of this book may be reproduced, stored, or transmitted by any means—whether auditory, graphic, mechanical, or electronic—without written permission of the author, except in the case of brief excerpts used in critical articles and reviews. Unauthorized reproduction of any part of this work is illegal and is punishable by law.

This e-book is licensed for your personal enjoyment only. This e-book may not be resold or given away to other people. If you'd like to share this book with another person, please purchase an additional copy for each person you share it with.

ISBN: 978-1-4834-6971-3 (sc)
ISBN: 978-1-4834-6970-6 (e)

Library of Congress Control Number: 2017907775

Because of the dynamic nature of the Internet, any web addresses or links contained in this book may have changed since publication and may no longer be valid. The views expressed in this work are solely those of the author and do not necessarily reflect the views of the publisher, and the publisher hereby disclaims any responsibility for them.

Any people depicted in stock imagery provided by Thinkstock are models, and such images are being used for illustrative purposes only.
Certain stock imagery © Thinkstock.

Lulu Publishing Services rev. date: 05/24/2017

To my sons, Laurence, Fernando and Adrian.
You are the best part of my journey.
All my love, Mom.

Contents

Prologue ix

Chapter 1   La Habana, September 1961 1

Chapter 2   Jamaica 12

Chapter 3   Miami 19

Chapter 4   Stamford 25

Chapter 5   New England Celebrations 35

Chapter 6   Translations 42

Chapter 7   New Beginnings 49

Chapter 8   Growing Older 54

Chapter 9   Return and Redemption 57

About the author 61

Prologue

My day begins like every other day, unremarkable in its sameness—but only on the surface. On this typical morning, as I go through the motions of my daily routine, nothing seems unusual, but underneath I am like a simmering pot that has reached the boiling point and whose lid may not contain the roiling water for much longer.

I stroll to the kitchen, not eager to feel the chill of the wintry air on my face. Peering through the window, I see the flat gray sameness of this February day in Connecticut. The weatherman said on the late-night news yesterday that it would be one of the coldest in 2016. To me, cold is cold, and the distinction is a vague attempt at making us forget that. But it is hard to ignore the feeling, when deep in your sixty-three-year-old bones you still faintly remember the warmth of that strong Cuban sun. Living in this land of icy winters since 1961 never erased my intense dislike of the cold and my longing for the heat of the tropics.

It is Laurence's birthday, my eldest son. He will be thirty-eight years old today. He hinted that he would like to have *frijoles colorados*, known here as kidney beans, as a part of his celebratory dinner, and of course I will make them for him. Remembering a Cuban song I learned long ago, I hum to myself as I open the cabinets and take out the ingredients for preparing the specialty meal.

I hold a large spanish onion in my hand and begin to peel away the layers. With each one, the stories in my head once again take hold of my mind as I stare out into the garden, looking at the gray landscape. The flowers that usually bloom here in the summer are either dead or fast asleep, waiting for spring to awaken them. The thoughts that rise up slowly in my mind are also waiting to bloom, and I am a little girl again, in the place where I was born, instead of a mature woman cooking in her well-worn kitchen. It is as if the chapters of my life are revealing themselves, one by one, and I am surrounded by the beauty of their colors and variety. I remember the people, places, sights, and sounds of a time long ago.

I do not light the scented candle in my kitchen today, for I want the pungent smell of the onion and the garlic and the bay leaf to transport me back in time to another kitchen, where a heavyset, pretty woman makes these identical preparations.

My grandmother—or, as we would say in Spanish, my *abuela*—taught me how to cook, and although I cannot match her innate skill, my feeble attempts to honor her are heartfelt. I think of those days with a smile, watching her artful preparations that belied the fact that she had very little schooling. I remember her telling me to get out of the kitchen and to go read my books. Words can only feed the soul in certain ways—sometimes you also need tangible memories.

I was born in 1953, the same year that the revolution began against then president Fulgencio Batista. Castro's July 26 movement got its name from this fateful date, which has signified so much suffering for the Cuban people. After years of guerrilla warfare, Castro came down from the hills and became the island's sole ruler and dictator. Batista left Cuba on January 1, 1959, and that marked the beginning of the end of life as we knew it. I remember the cheering and the parades because many people thought this bearded savior was the answer to all their prayers. But many others saw the writing on the wall and fled, leaving behind everything they had ever known and loved, including family. Recently, the US president issued an order lifting the travel restrictions on Cuba that had been in place many years. The news was met with mixed reactions throughout the Cuban-exile community. Some welcomed the opportunity to return, while others cursed the day and vowed never to set foot on the island until it was free from Communist rule, invoking promises to those who had died here having never had the chance to see their birthplace again.

I have lovingly continued to slice throughout my reverie and find a pile of perfectly concentric circles on the cutting board in front of me. My face is wet with tears, and I wipe away at them with the back of my hand, knowing full well the power of a spanish onion.

Chapter 1

La Habana, September 1961

It was a typical morning, sun shining, tropical breeze, with just a hint of that *aire de agua*, or "rain wind," whispering of the rain that would most likely fall later in the day. I had been awake for a few hours, not understanding the reason why we were leaving. Over the past months, I had tried to listen to the hushed tones of my parents in the middle of the night when they discussed our exodus. I was never able to make out what was being said and was too fearful to ask them directly why we were planning to go. All I knew was that on this day, we were leaving La Habana.

The situation in Cuba was not exactly favorable for its middle-class citizens. They were seen as the haves in a world that now favored the have-nots. Property was being seized, and citizens were routinely rounded up, accused of crimes against the revolution. Many of the people we knew had already left. In our family, the fear was palpable, as my father had been a policeman and my grandfather was in the military. Almost immediately after the taking of La Habana, plans were set in motion for us to leave the island. My seven-year-old self wished and hoped that things would be fine and we would stay in La Habana after all. But that was not to be, and every part of me knew that the day had finally arrived. There was no going back.

La Habana was the capital of Cuba. It had been my island home for all my short years, and I loved everything about it. I looked forward to the rare days when Ramon was off from work and would take me to the Paseo del Malecon, the popular strolling place by the bay. I was awed by the powerful waves that hit the rock wall, as well as by the Castillo del Morro, the aging castle, standing in the distance, a steadfast reminder of our somewhat dark maritime history.

Only the month before, I had caught an eye-opening glimpse of the present troubles. It had been the start of an exciting day, and I remember that Abuelo, my grandfather, and I walked briskly toward the big tent at the Orbay y Cerrato, a popular furniture warehouse a few blocks from our home, where seasonal circuses enticed both young and old. Midway through the exciting sights and sounds of the event, the familiar figure of my great-aunt Margot suddenly appeared in the aisle and whispered to Abuelo. He stood up suddenly and led me to the exit. We walked in silence, but the stony look on his face in addition to the few hushed murmurs between the adults told me there was trouble.

As we arrived at our door, I was startled by the presence of a *miliciano*, one of the ubiquitous military soldiers, standing guard, rifle in hand. Margot had left us a block or so before, as her task as messenger of doom had been completed. Abuelo brought me inside the house and was promptly escorted out, this time led brusquely by the arm and held in a tight grip by one of the two militia men who had been waiting for him in the apartment. Abuela paced furiously, and before she could embrace me in a greeting, she went and stood by the open door of my mother's bedroom, where the second soldier, gun at the ready, prepared to enter. Eyes blazing and fearless, she blocked the door and yelled that he was not here—"No esta aquí!"—and continued in her authoritative voice, telling him that her daughter was a sick, frail woman and to let her be. He spun on his heel, shoving Abuela out of the way as he headed for the front door, which he slammed with frustration on his way out at the realization that they would not arrest my father that day for his affiliation with the police department of the former regime. Little did we know that he was already being interrogated at the station, a part of the day's routine roundup of people believed to be against the state. I entered my mother's room, where Abuela fussed with the pillows and hovered over my mother's ashen face, alternately offering words of comfort to her and uttering heartfelt curses to the now-departed intruders.

As I closed my eyes, trying to shut my mind off from reality, I remembered my school and my friends. Ramon, being a staunch Roman Catholic, had insisted that I attend one of the private religious schools in the capital. We were far from well-to-do, but I was the only child in the family, and he wanted the absolute best schooling for me. I had a couple of good friends who attended the same school. We usually rotated visits on weekends since I was rarely allowed distractions on school days. The time Dania and Maria Luisa and I spent together was magical. We played dolls, jumped rope, heard fabulous stories from Abuelo, and sometimes we strolled to the corner fruit market with Abuela. The market was owned by a Chinese family, and they had the freshest and loveliest fruit for sale. I was still in my bed and already missing them. It was very difficult to comprehend that I might not see them the coming weekend. I would never see them again, for they both passed away during my years in exile.

As I rolled over, I sighed, trying to imagine life without Abuela. Although Ramon had tried to convince me that she and Abuelo would join us in a short time, to me "a short time" was relative. I wanted the particular date and time when my grandparents would be with us. My grandparents had always been there for me. Abuela, especially, left her indelible mark. Her ways were quite different from the ways of those around her, and she was fiery, independent, and fiercely loyal. She believed in traditional roles and lived by the rules of her Santeria practices, Cuban beliefs rooted in African gods and goddesses, to the chagrin of Ramon. No matter how much he tried to change her views, it was not worth the trouble. There had been an argument just the day before about my helping out in the kitchen instead of simply spending the day reading or playing with my friends. Ramon curtly informed her that he would not watch his only child have a life of endless toil, devoid of intellect and joy.

"She will be a flower to be cultivated and not a weed to be pulled," he said with his fists clenched in anger.

Abuela exhaled sharply, walked away, and shook her head, wondering how I was ever to be a future wife and mother if she could not teach me the needed skills. My mother had learned to be a passive spectator during these conflicts. She cheered neither party, always feigning illness, as she left the room without looking back.

I was getting restless, yet I was not ready to face the activities of the day. Leaving the home I had grown to cherish was heartbreaking. Everything would be lost now that my parents had decided to flee to an unknown country. I was told very little but knew we were going to fly somewhere on an airplane. I was clearly instructed to not ever speak of this to anyone, and I carried the secret in my head like a glass bird, so afraid it would somehow fall and shatter. Had we been discovered, and our plan to vacation revealed for what it was, there would have been dire consequences. Looking back on that eventful time, it is clear to me now how much of a risk my parents were taking in plotting to escape from Communist Cuba so soon after Fidel Castro took power and began to rule with a fist every bit as tyrannical as Batista's, if not more so.

We lived in an apartment in a modern, six-story building. It was generously apportioned with three bedrooms, and it was airy and light, with a large balcony. I had my own room, Ramon and Herminia, my parents, had theirs, and the last was for Abuela and Abuelo. Although sometimes I wished I had a little sister I could play with when I was all alone in my room at night, that was not meant to be, at least not in La Habana. I found out many years later that my mother, always frail and sickly in her youth, had suffered a series of miscarriages during her childbearing years. Abuelo and Abuela had always lived with us, mostly due to my mother's frequent illnesses. I once heard Abuelo say that he thanked God every day for allowing her to live as long as she had. This made me doubt the possibility of ever having a sibling, but the mysteries of life are many, as my only sister was born when I was twelve years old and my mother lived well past the age of ninety.

Abuela was the first to come into my room that morning, and she was holding a glass of warm *café con leche*, the traditional coffee with milk we had each day for breakfast, and telling me that it was time to get up. Opening my eyes, I tried to mumble a greeting in her direction as she systematically drew the curtains, exposing the brilliant Cuban sun, which shone in all its glory onto my sleepy face. I didn't want to leave the warmth and comfort of my bed, and she gave me a look that said, "Now." I climbed out reluctantly and prepared to start my sojourn out of La Habana. My dress and shoes were carefully laid out. The dress was beautiful, a well-pressed cotton gingham with little flowers embroidered along the wide hem. It had been hand-sewn by Abuela, as were all the others.

Abuela was a gifted woman. She was so creative with her hands! Sometimes I wondered how she was able to do all the things she did. Her cooking was cuisine level. I always looked forward to her frijoles colorados, the red beans that were one of the many recipes that she confessed had healing powers. Abuela never bought dresses for herself; she made them. One day she explained to me how important it was to make your own clothes, after I asked her why she didn't buy dresses like my friend Maria Luisa's Abuela who had come to visit last Christmas. In her strong voice, she told me how she was unable to afford store prices but emphasized how much she had been able to save over the years by making her own clothes on her beloved sewing machine. Her eyes beamed when she remarked how special her clothes were because no one else had them. The machine, an old model with a black iron pedal, was a staple of my childhood memory, as was the sight of her head bent over, gently guiding the fabric under the bobbing needle. I remember promising to buy her a dress from a fancy shop someday, and she laughed and told me a little story. I can still hear her voice all these years later as she told me that tale. I was sitting on her bed, my feet not touching the floor. It was one of those hot, sultry, humid nights when the Caribbean easterlies washed over the island and brought no relief.

"I will tell you a story," Abuela said. "I was walking in the center of the city on my way to Flogar. You know Flogar?" she asked. I nodded. Everyone knew Flogar; it was one of the best-known stores in La Habana. "So, as I was walking in downtown La Habana I was dressed for the occasion, and I wore one of my better creations, not my signature *delantar*."

I smiled because I knew that this was her apron, the fashion staple of Cuban homemakers. She winked at me and continued. "The streets were crowded that day, and as I crossed the main street and stepped up on the curb, I looked up and saw the image of a woman in the glass case of one of the many along the sidewalk, displaying varied wares."

She cocked her head a little and said, "So, I thought to myself, *What a lovely lady*, and in an instant I realized I had been looking at my own reflection!" Letting out her strong, melodic laugh, she looked at me and said in a firm voice, "Always remember that clothes are important, and if they make you unique, make you stand out from the crowd, then they become the stamp of who you are in the world." I stood up and walked to the bathroom, where I tried to memorize the pattern of the small, shiny blue tiles. As I passed the lone, tiny suitcase that held the few belongings I was allowed to bring, tears rushed down my face, and it hit me that we had no plans of ever coming back to La Habana. I succeeded in turning my face from Abuela as she went through the ritual of preparing my bath for me. Unlike most of my friends, I did not bathe myself. Abuela felt I was much too young to do this properly, so she took it upon herself to do the honors, as though I were still a baby. I think back on my grandmother's care of me, now that I am grown, with children of my own, and I see that perhaps all her coddling had deeper implications. She had seen her daughter grow sick from the time she was a child, and I believe she saw in me hope for the future of our family—someone strong, like her, for the next generation.

Bathed and dressed for the long journey, I went to the kitchen for breakfast. When I saw Abuelo, I gave him a tight hug and a kiss on the cheek. Abuelo was a quiet man. He had once been in the army, and I always had the feeling that he had a lot to say but felt the world would not be able to handle the information. He was tall, lean, kindly, religious, and highly intelligent. He returned my kiss, and we ate the light meal in silence. As I waited in the small, familiar living room that I had grown to love, and stared at the pictures that hung on the walls, I could hear the commotion as my parents prepared to leave for the airport. We were leaving Cuba on an airplane bound for Jamaica, supposedly for a few days of relaxation on the beach. My father, Ramon, was *alterado*, on high alert, and ticking off every detail, lest we forget any of the important documents needed for our trip. Herminia was listless, and her hooded eyes held the sadness she felt in every fiber of her being that day. Abuelo was somber and reserved, but Abuela, as always, provided the strength that every member of the family needed but could not conjure.

Abuela's firm voice could be heard through every room in the apartment as she directed everyone and argued with Ramon, openly invoking Santa Barbara and all her saints, to the great annoyance of my father, who had once studied in the seminary to become a priest. Theirs had always been a tentative relationship, a little war with frequent ceasefires that did not last for long.

We were all on the sidewalk saying our goodbyes when I remembered I had forgotten something. As I ran toward the house, I could feel my mother's vacant look on my back. I had forgotten the small coral bracelet from my last birthday. When I emerged, Abuela smiled when she saw what I held in my hand. I could almost see her eyes glistering with tears, but she quickly waved her emotions away and fastened the bracelet onto my tiny wrist.

I barely recall the actual moment of leave-taking, except for the brief but fierce hug I gave Abuela at the door of the apartment as we prepared to board the taxicab. I waved till we got to the bend in the road that led to the main avenue, and I could not see the familiar figures anymore. The journey to the airport was uneventful, with everyone obviously thinking of the unforeseen future. My parents did not say a word, and I kept silent as well. About an hour later, we approached the entrance to the Rancho Boyeros Airport. There were military personnel with visible weapons standing guard. I was walking beside my parents, and I saw my father grab my mother's hand.

We walked hesitantly toward the line to be checked in, and I made sure to keep my eyes down and not speak a word, as I had been instructed earlier that morning. Check-in took a while, and I was getting thirsty from the heat on a journey that had not truly started. I made no complaint to my mother, for I was a perceptive little girl, and the fear and uncertainty I saw in her face immediately erased my need for water as we progressed slowly and the line moved forward, seemingly inch by inch.

There were so many rules: no family to see us off, one suitcase per person, no currency, no jewelry, no religious artifacts, and the list went on and on. I stood before a middle-aged woman with a hard face who was to check the women and children for unacceptable items. I took a few steps toward her as I watched my father being checked in by a uniformed man. She told me to stretch out my arms, which I did, still not looking at her face. Immediately, she noticed the little coral bracelet that I wore, and she grabbed my arm and made an attempt to remove it. I flinched, stepped back, and started to cry. This was one thing I had to take with me, I told myself, and not even this woman with a hard face could take it away from me. In that defining moment, this entire story could have had a different ending. I will never know why she stared at me and said, "chiquilla malcriada," Spanish for "spoiled brat," with a disgusted grimace and roughly let go of my arm, which was still sore from the effects of the varicella vaccine I had received a few weeks before and almost cost me my life. Then she waved me on. One of the most difficult memories I have is of the obligatory vaccination everyone who was leaving Cuba in those days was required to have. We stood in the hot sun, in a long line. I recall tables covered in plastic, behind which could be seen a group of doctors and nurses. As the line inched forward, I could see trays holding syringes with long, pointy needles. I had been well schooled before leaving the house that morning, and my abuela held me firmly by the hand. She had been clear that I was not to cry or make a fuss, no matter what they did. She had cut a lemon in half and put it in her bag before we left. The nurse who pulled at my arm to inject the serum held the needle down, pushed it deep into my bicep, and moved it in a circular motion. The pain and terror were too much to for me to bear. I howled in agony as my Abuela dragged me quickly away and then took the lemon half and squeezed it on the round, red welt and held it there for what seemed an eternity. Once home, my arm continued to throb well into the night, and then the fever started. I was delirious for two days, and the welt on my arm got bigger and bigger. Now a boil had formed, which ruptured and left a pus-filled, bloody crater in my arm. I still carry the reminder, visible on the rare occasions when I am sleeveless.

The airplane was a new and frightening experience. At first I was joyful about being on an airplane because I had never been on one before. As soon as we climbed the stairs into the plane, Ramon tried to calm me down because he could sense my excitement in the way I was beaming at the enormous aircraft. The outside of the plane was bright and shiny, a futuristic promise standing on the runway at the ready to take me to adventures unknown. But soon that light and heady feeling turned dark as I stood at the door and peered in. As we entered the plane I looked down the long tunnel of seats and was swept by a cold and sudden fear. The round, tight, dimly lit tube was oppressive, and the small windows offered no relief from the feeling of being caged, like a little bird in the rough grip of a large hand. My breathing became rapid, and I could feel beads of sweat on my forehead. I could not bear the claustrophobia and made a run back to the door, to the open island air, to my home, to my

Abuela … but the stewardess was knowledgeable and kind, and with a soft, firm hand, she gently guided me to my seat, giving me one of those little plastic pins that said "KLM Airlines." Her touch made the bubble of tension that had lived in my chest all morning burst. It felt like that last drop of water dropped on the surface of a penny. I held fast to my copy of *Las Mil y Una Noches*, the well-known *One Thousand and One Nights*, the book that had been my farewell gift from Abuelo, for the entire flight. The stewardess came to check on me few times to make sure I was okay, and Ramon assured her I was. Toward the end of the journey, she brought me some biscuits and told me in accented Spanish that her name was Enna and that she was from Amsterdam.

We traveled with a few people from La Habana, most of them unfamiliar faces. Ramon did not seem interested in associating with people on this journey, as we were not yet in the clear, so I took my cue from him, paying attention to just my parents and avoiding contact with the passengers from Cuba. I recall seeing a little girl of about six with soft, blue eyes in the aisle across from us. I have always been fascinated by people with light eyes, blue, green … and when I was small, I often wondered how they were able to see. I was getting a little bored, and even to this avid reader, Abuelo's book began to lose its luster. I wanted someone to play with, and my parents were somber and engrossed in their thoughts. I looked at Herminia, who had begun to nod off, and then shifted my gaze to Ramon for permission to engage the little girl, but got none.

Smiling to myself, I assumed Ramon's silence meant consent, so I started talking with the little girl on the plane. Her name was Marisol, and she said they were going on vacation (this is what everyone assumed my family was doing as well), and my heart sank, knowing that, like me, she had been forced to leave her little life behind. Not everyone who left under false pretenses made it out of Cuba, as Castro did not allow citizens to simply leave the island. This journey held hidden peril, for if we were found out, we feared we'd be sent back, and that meant certain death. But we were the lucky ones, leaving on an airplane, heading for that elusive "vacation destination." Others left in desperation by means that would eventually cost them their lives, like the many souls who rest at the bottom of the ocean, having attempted escape in makeshift rafts and rickety boats.

Ramon shifted his gaze to me and I could feel his eyes poring through my back, so I quickly smiled at the little girl, shyly waved, and turned back to my book, ready to keep quiet for the rest of the journey. We finally arrived at our destination in Kingston, Jamaica, and it was a relief to be out of the enclosed chamber at last. As we alighted, I saw Marisol walking away with her family. She turned to smile at me, and I waved back. I would never see her again. My consolation came as I felt the sun warm on my shoulders and thought how much it felt like the one I had left behind.

Chapter 2

Jamaica

The humidity was high and the airless bus stifling as we slowly made our way down an unfamiliar road. I could not make out how many people were on the bus, but it was crowded. The unpleasant body odor and the complaints of passengers over space made the ride hellish. I was hot and sleepy when we arrived at our destination, and I had to be carried the half block or so to the entrance and down the gravel driveway. We were in Kingston, Jamaica, and a man called Mr. Sahmuel greeted us as we climbed the steps to the enormous wraparound porch of the house that he owned. We had been referred by our contacts in Cuba and were now joined by a few family members who had also left the island. From Ramon's side, we met an uncle and aunt who were childless and from Herminia's side, a first cousin and his son, who was four years older than me.

Within few minutes of our arrival, a maid who had helped prepare our quarters motioned for us to follow her up a wide, curved staircase, and she led us through a narrow hallway to the room we had been assigned. I was placed on a small bed in the dimly lit room once everything was arranged and the maid had taken her leave. The room was cooled only by an old, whirring ceiling fan.

My mother's face was lined with concern as she realized I was once again sick and had to see a doctor. Illness had been a constant companion in my early years, and the long trip and the stress brought on the usual symptoms. My forehead continued to burn, and my father went outside to seek assistance. Muted voices in the room were barely audible as I succumbed to the delirium of the fever. The doctor came after what seemed like an eternity, and it was many years later that I learned that he only agreed to see me if we paid him in American dollars, a rare commodity for Cuban refugees. He asked my parents a few questions in imperfect Spanish and gave me an injection. My father was charged the expected one hundred dollars for the brief visit. Little did I know that it was a king's ransom. It was all the money we had, having been smuggled out in the heels of my father's shoes, rolled up in little tubes. Had this been discovered, we would have been prohibited from leaving, and my father would most likely have been shot.

My mother had been oblivious to the cargo inside my father's shoes and was horrified to learn of its existence, knowing the likely consequences. She took to her bed for two days with one of her blinding migraines. Unsurprisingly, there was no argument about this later on. It was simply brushed aside, just another chapter in the saga of silent resignation that had become our fate—the dark mystery that was now our reality.

We soon found out that the beds were treacherous territory in this particular establishment, for a few days later, my mother had the same infernal rash that had overtaken my arms and legs after the fever had broken. At first my parents thought it was a side effect of my illness, but others in the refugee group were also displaying these red, itchy welts. The source was well known to the servants, who told us they were *chinchas*, or bedbugs, and common in the bedrooms of the house. They then took the mattresses away to be burned.

The first night after the mattress was burned, we had to sleep on pieces of thick cloth. Herminia grumbled, silently chiding Ramon for listening to the relatives who convinced him this place would be a safe haven on our way to the United States.

The next morning, we woke to the news that mattresses would be brought to our room, and although they were not new, they were free from bugs and definitely preferred to the pieces of thick cloth we had slept on the night before and had caused our joints to ache that morning.

The building that housed us was a once well-appointed, if decaying, halfway house. It sat between the main road and the ocean. Several female servants scurried about with lowered heads and a quick step, giving hesitant sideways glances when a command was barked in their direction and not one of them daring to look Mr. Sahmuel directly in the eye. We saw them every morning in the dining room, where they set before us plates of grey balls of starchy, boiled, cassava-like *aki* for our meals. There was only tea to drink (we only had tea when we had stomach ills in Cuba, as coffee was king). We could not get the food down and for the first few days drank tea with condensed milk and ate dry crackers.

A big man with a ruddy complexion and steely blue eyes, Mr. Sahmuel, despite his girth, walked with a swaggering step and kept his gun well holstered and tucked into his expansive waistband. He had little interaction with his houseguests, but I do remember one special afternoon when my father and a couple of the other refugees went for a brief ride on his boat. I was feeling much better by then, and I had pleaded with my father to come along, ignoring my mother's protestations that, like her, I could not swim. Mr. Sahmuel nodded and in the flawless Spanish he occasionally spoke, told Ramon to bring me along.

The journey to the boat was quite a distance. Our motley crew consisted of Mr. Sahmuel, my father, my uncle, my mother's cousin, and his son. I was glaringly out of place in this manly group but stayed quiet and out of the way, all the while secretly delighted to be included in this unexpected adventure. We rode to the small marina in a car with no air-conditioning, and although the ride was stuffy and uncomfortable, we certainly fared better than the few people we passed along the way, who walked wearily under the merciless late-morning sun. I tried to focus on the natural beauty of the passing Jamaican landscape and saw lush trees and colorful flowers along the dirt road leading to the clear blue ocean. I was momentarily reminded of the many rides we had taken to the ocean back in Cuba, where we spent lovely days at the shore. Those had been very different from what I was experiencing today, with sleek classic cars interspersed with the horse and buggies loved by the American and European tourists. But there was a familiar similarity in the landscape, the sun, and the sea, and it comforted me like a warm embrace. We eventually arrived at the dock and saw the boat. It was a good-sized wooden powerboat named *Maria*. Mr. Sahmuel told us the boat was named after someone he had loved dearly. We did not understand why he would share this information with us; it was as if he'd been thinking aloud. I could not look away from the glistening diamonds on the surface of the clear blue water. Once we were aboard, the engine sputtered to life, and we began to move away from the shore. I was mesmerized by the natural beauty of the vast ocean before me and inhaled deeply the salty smell of the tropical sea. The boat ride consisted of a lot of talking and maritime explanation from Mr. Sahmuel, and we were his captive audience. He showed us parts of the beautiful Jamaican coastline and even offered us small bottles of cola halfway through the ride from a cooler he kept well stocked. We returned to the dock that afternoon, and I was once again tired and on my father's shoulders. It was an interesting day, and George, the son of my mother's cousin, and I made friends while out on the open sea. Years later, he always owned a boat. I wonder if he heard the siren call of the sea for the first time that day all those years ago.

Herminia was frantic with worry due to our late return and was not eager to hear the details of our boat ride. Shortly after we arrived at the house, the maids had dinner served, and we had a much-improved meal. My eyes danced with anticipation when I saw the familiar rosy hue of the red snappers being placed in platters in the center of the long table.

As we prepared to sleep that night, Ramon gave Herminia unsolicited details of the boat ride, and she listened in silence. I put my head in my palms, ready to sleep, only to discover that Ramon was explaining something about the boat's name—Maria. He was telling a story of his days in the seminary and of his devotion to the Virgen Maria, the Virgin Mary. Every day his spirituality grew, and he made a promise that he would honor this name forever. I was feeling more and more sleepy but managed to stay awake long enough to hear that many years later, after his departure from the seminary, when he and Herminia had been married and wishing for a child, he vowed that if it was a girl, her name would be Maria. I later found out that my mother believed the name to be too common, so Ramon convinced her to accept the Hebrew version of the name that he had come to know from his study of the Bible, so they named me Miriam. He had been moved that day as he boarded the boat and seen the name. To him it had been a sign from God Himself that we would all be held in the palm of His hand throughout this tumultuous journey filled with fear and the unknown. I finally drifted off to sleep dreaming about the ocean, my father, and a boat that shared my name.

We were in Jamaica for thirteen days before we took another flight, this time to Miami. Our travels were a little like the Underground Railroad, where people helped one another for a common end, which was freedom. My father had little money, but he had saved enough to pay for part of the plane tickets. The stay in Jamaica and our brief stay in Miami were funded by family and friends, our benefactors in the United States. On the last day of our stay at Mr. Sahmuel's, I was helping Herminia to pack our few things into our small suitcases. Ramon had gone for a walk with the men, as there had been some trouble near the house. She started talking almost to herself and asked if I knew my father had been destined to be a reverend. I was shocked beyond words. I knew the story of my parents' meeting, but it had never been a topic of conversation that included me. Perhaps in the absence of the women of the family who had always been her support, Herminia needed me to speed up the process of growing up and begin to join her circle. That was the slow start of my adulthood, and to this day I know more about this family, good and bad, than any of its members.

Ramon was born into a family of seven children. Theirs was a close-knit family, and they were poor as church mice. Herminia was the only child of her parents, but unlike Ramon (who had the freedom to do as he pleased while growing up), Herminia was very sheltered as a child. She never left her parents and was fully dependent on them, even after she met Ramon.

Herminia had attended the school in Matanzas, one of Cuba's seven provinces and her birthplace, and Ramon was born and bred in Trinidad, one of La Habana's poorer neighborhoods. Given the challenge of feeding seven children, it was decided that Ramon and two of his brothers would be enrolled at the Catholic Seminary of El Buen Pastor, the Good Shepherd. At that time, he was a devout student with every intention of entering the priesthood.

Years passed, and the two of them might as well have been ships in the night, but for a chance meeting. Herminia had become the organist of the church in the town where she lived. Around the same time, Ramon was ordered to Matanzas to minister to the parish, in the absence of one of the priests who had become ill, and also in preparation for the finalization of his journey toward the priesthood.

Herminia then recalled a particular mass during which she had played the organ. Ramon walked up to her after mass and complimented her musical abilities. He introduced himself and was friendly and cordial. Her response was guarded, as she did not want to send wrong signals. It took a while for Ramon to finally voice his intentions, and immediately afterward, he requested a release from the seminary.

Herminia was reluctant to marry Ramon at first, feeling she was the reason he had left the seminary. Ramon was able to convince her that being married to her did not hinder his working for God, and this was a true fact, as he spent the last twenty-eight years of his life as an ordained deacon of the Catholic Church, ministering to the sick, the suffering, and the lost. They had a lovely wedding and honeymooned on the coast, amazingly enough as a gift from one of the seminary heads who had taken a fatherly role in Ramon's life since their initial meeting. My parents were married for almost sixty years, and they were an inseparable couple, both in good and bad times.

Chapter 3

Miami

Two weeks to the day of our arrival in Jamaica, we were on an airplane again. This time our destination was Miami, and I was again fearful and nostalgic at the prospect of another new place that was not my home. I sat by the window this time, with traces of my previous claustrophobia still lurking. I looked down at the puffy white clouds in awe, making out shapes and images from my imagination and pulling on my father's sleeve to confirm my growing menagerie of gauzy birds, animals, and fish. I looked at the stewardesses as they walked through the cabin and was struck by their beauty. They were stylishly dressed and perfectly coiffed and resembled magazine models. I wondered if they enjoyed their gypsy lives and were not fazed by having to travel so much. When we landed, I sighed with relief and then took in a little breath of air, suddenly realizing this was not La Habana.

I could barely recall any of the details of our transport, conversations, or persons we saw at that time. The carousel of memory only gave me one brass ring, and that was the brief walk down a residential street en route to an uncle's house. The same little patent-leather white shoes in which I took my last steps on Cuban soil now propelled me along the sidewalk, holding on to my mother's hand. A small tickle on my calf suddenly grew more noticeable, and I looked down to see an enormous *cucaracha*, the native palmetto bug, climbing up my leg. Frozen in place, I let out several bloodcurdling screams. My mother tried to pull me along, to no avail. Seeing no rescue coming, I shook my leg hard and swatted the insect with the back of my hand. Welcome to Miami, little Miriam.

A bit later, once at my uncle's house, I began to feel at home. We ate delicious and familiar food, and I could have sworn that the Formica table and chairs were the same as the ones we had back in Cuba.

The family members who had stayed at the house with us in Kingston had all come with us to Miami on the same flight. There had been a sense of urgency to leave the island after fourteen days because there were elections being held. There had been many threats made to us by dreadlocked Rastafarian men riding bicycles along the main road, in front of the house, holding their fingers to their throats and slicing the air. There were shivers of terror at the thought that their party would win the upcoming elections and that they would come back to make good on their promise. On our last night in the rooming house, I fell asleep to the hushed tones of my parents discussing what three of the Cuban men had done that evening. Tired of the taunts and the threats, they had waited in hiding near the gate for the men to pass by on their bicycles. One trailed behind, and he was ambushed and beaten and his bicycle all but destroyed. There was a sickening sense that retribution for this act would rain down on all the Cuban residents staying there, and a decision had been made to leave early the next morning. So, once again enveloped in fear, our small group left together after a final trip to the embassy. We were transported by taxicab that morning and rode to the airport, relieved that we had escaped traveling in the hot, rickety, foul-smelling bus that had brought us in only a few days prior.

We did not see my father for several days after our arrival in Miami. He had gone, with a few of the others, to Opa-Locka to be "processed." This meant that the United States wanted to be sure that he was really a refugee and not a spy for the Cuban government. Of course, I knew nothing of this, as I was told nothing and knew better than to ask. But

I remember my father later told us that the processing was a frightening experience, and that it was a very serious and defining event. If you were singled out because of any discovered previous Communist activity, you were immediately pulled from the group to be sent back to the island. My father was cleared because there was nothing in any government file tying him to any of the above. He did mention that one of the men was not truthful about previous activity, and they had a file with photos showing him in a pro-Castro rally. He was immediately slotted for return, as the processing itself was judge and jury, and was then most likely shot on arrival for having attempted to escape in the first place. My father returned, to the immense relief of the family. Life in Cuba in the early days of the Castro regime was unpredictable and frightening. Decisions were made on the whims of those in power, from the unforgiving members of the neighborhood *comites*, or committees, to those in higher echelons of power. Violence was rampant, and the only television station allowed depicted the daily slayings of those thought to be against the revolution with merciless repetition. The long, blank wall known as the Paredon, or firing squad wall, was given a fresh coat of blood every day, as hapless men, many of them innocent, stood blindfolded and terrified as they were felled by the hail of bullets. The *rat-tat-tat* of the rapidly firing guns became the soundtrack of our television viewing, silenced only when the loud, dictatorial voice of El Comandante, the Commander, gave a few hours of relief from death, replacing it with one of his many *discursos*, the long, ranting political speeches to which we were regularly subjected.

For the few days we were in Miami, we stayed at the uncle's house. By the third day after our arrival in Miami, I was bored with staying indoors but did not dare to venture outside due to the recently induced trauma brought on by the local insects. I sat listlessly with the small pad of paper and handful of colored pencils I was given to draw. I later learned that the "uncle" and his kindly wife were really loyal, longtime friends of Ramon and Herminia. It was not unusual in our culture for friends to become family with the passage of time. They had left the island earlier than we had, sensing the trouble that eventually did arrive.

As I drew, I listened intently as Herminia engaged in conversation with my "aunt." There was a story about to be told, and they had my full attention, as listening to adult talk was my sport of choice—a defiant response to the repressive custom that shut me out from being included due to my age. We were not allowed as spectators into any conversation, much less participants. The familiar saying "Los ninos hablan cuando las gallinas mean" summed up when Cuban children were allowed to speak, and in translation it meant "when hens pee"—thus, never.

The story went like this: A friend of my aunt's lived in Cuba with her husband and four children. They did not sympathize with the new government, unlike many of their neighbors who also lived in the small town in the countryside and were of modest means. They could not afford to leave the island, as some had, by airplane. They were too afraid to venture out over the ocean by boat, as many had tried to do and as a result, found their resting place at the bottom of the sea. So they hatched a plan to have the husband escape through the swamps at the western end of the island and to send the two oldest children, both girls, out through a new program being offered called Pedro Pan in America. Children were sent to the United States to stay with host families or in centers until their parents could join them. It was a charitable effort that yielded mixed results.

I silently gasped at the thought that this could have easily happened to me and continued to eavesdrop, my little heart beating a mile a minute. The girls were temporarily placed in an orphanage in the south of the United States, and the father, after a harrowing escape, made it to shore and began the laborious process of reclaiming his family. A few years passed, and the father finally reunited with the family. It was then that the tales of horror emerged. The father had lost a limb in a struggle with a vicious crocodile in the treacherous Cienaga Zapata, the vast Zapata Swamp, and the mother, along with her young sons, who was left behind, experienced the usual taunts and degradation freely given to those thought to be against the current regime, not to mention hunger, loneliness, and the desperation of being separated from her family, not knowing if she would see her husband and daughters again. The girls fared no better. They were young and pretty and thoroughly despised by the sadistic nuns who were in charge of caring for them. They were "corrected" for any minute infraction, a pseudonym for physical abuse. The girls had lovely, long brown hair, and when they spent a minute too long caring for it, they would be beaten with the very brush they used to untangle it. One particular day, in a fit of rage, the nun in charge of the dormitory took a pair of scissors to them both, and in the end, their hair covered the cold tile floor like a carpet. I closed my eyes in terror and wished I had not listened so intently to the adults that afternoon.

After hearing their story, I hoped to meet them someday, and my heart ached for them as I imagined what they must have gone through living in those conditions. With fear written all over my face, I returned to my drawing, silently thanking God for my parents and for sparing me from a similar fate.

So far, the places where we had stopped were akin to the place where I was born. The air was hot and humid, palm trees dotted the landscape, and pretty flowers of many colors trailed everywhere. The people around me spoke in Spanish, and the food we ate was palatable and familiar. The blue sky and bright yellow sun comforted me like a soft and well-worn blanket.

Today, I recall little of our Miami stay. We were in a small house with people who were like family. It seemed that everyone went out often, for one thing or another, and most times I stayed in with Herminia. Ramon was usually not at home, and I saw little of him. We always walked. The temperature was warm, and I remember feeling at home there. I continue to feel this way every time I visit Florida (which I do often), and I think it is because it reminds me of Cuba.

When you are seven years old and not fully cognizant of experiencing trauma and loss, time is a fleeting shadow, a ghost you can tentatively see but cannot touch. The reality was that we were in Miami for five days, but to me it felt like many, many more. Then it was time to fly again, to board yet another plane for another, this time unfamiliar, destination. I missed my grandparents but was comforted by the presence of my mother and father. We landed in a place that was so foreign that this time I had no doubt that we had now arrived in the United States.

Chapter 4

Stamford

Our new location was so strikingly different from all the places we had previously been that this time I did not have to ask my parents where we were. Stamford was our final destination, and we arrived in the dead of night. I woke up the next morning and was so fatigued that I found it very difficult to move my legs due to the familiar and painful *calambres,* or cramps, I suffered from the age of five. Outside the room I had shared with my parents the night before, I could hear the gratingly shrill voice of my great-aunt Enriqueta as she talked through the closed door at my parents in her rapid rate of speech. I did not hear any response from my parents, except acquiescence, and I was not surprised. We were eternally grateful to her and to her sister, Micaela, for sponsoring us, so no matter what they said or did, we humbly and politely listened and accepted. I caught drift of the soliloquy, whose theme was basically the infinite perils of living in the United States. I understood but snippets of what was being said, yet came away with a fear of illness, as she exclaimed in high-pitched tones that getting sick in America was the equivalent of doom. I later discovered that all her words were an exaggeration designed to frighten the newcomers.

I did not leave the room but walked quietly to the window to avoid making any noise that would rouse her suspicions that I was already awake. Looking out the window, I saw that everything here was very different from the landscapes I had previously been accustomed to. The houses were two, sometimes three levels, and they were very similar in structure. Everything seemed to have been there for a long time, and the colors were washed out and tired. The only things that claimed to be alive were the trees. They were full and gloriously colored in their autumnal red and gold this late September. I had never seen anything so beautiful. Little did I know that it was their swan song, a final performance before the long, cold, hard winter that was to come.

I stepped back into the reality of the small room. I ventured downstairs a few minutes later, to discover that everyone but my mother had gone out. She was helping to tidy up the house. Her efforts were heartfelt, but she was not schooled in the details of housekeeping, and Abuela defended this to her death, always pointing out that she had given birth to a frail and sickly daughter who needed to conserve her strength to merely stay alive.

Menial work was the new taskmaster, and everything my father did for years to come revolved around it. There was daily worry about money, and Ramon took any and all jobs that were offered to him. From washing dishes to washing floors, to an assortment of factory jobs, nothing was outside the boundaries of what he would do to earn money for his family. His work in the local hotels ensured that we always had plenty of food, so I never experienced hunger. He was an outstanding provider, and even in the initial days after our arrival, when we knew lean times, he made sure that we were warm and fed. Years later I finally understood his vision, but in those days I just missed him, seeing him only on Sundays for church and an occasional paseo to visit my aunt in New York.

I saw Herminia take a break from her labors and sit by the window, expressionless, and with unfamiliar tears rolling down her cheeks. This sadness never left her, and she was listless for weeks, until the eventual arrival of her parents. An only child herself, mothering and nurturing was unfamiliar territory, and she only knew how to be cared for. I tried my best to console her, though I had no idea why she was crying. I sought solace in studying the landscape of this new place since I had no books to read, and they were my only comfort. The strange character of this new environment, where unbeknownst to me I would spend the bulk of my life, fascinated my young and curious mind. I watched few people walk down the street, so very different from the constant bustle of pedestrians back in La Habana. The houses were made of wood, were mostly white, but some had a red or green color, and they all had a second or third floor, and many had an attic. I remembered the cool facades of the buildings in Cuba, mostly concrete and light colored, as well as the homes in some of the *repartos* or developments, which were mostly ranch homes. The familiar palm trees and gardens had now been replaced with maple and elm trees, and the ground cover was mostly brownish grass. Across the street, there were little gold pom-pom flowers in the front garden, which I thought so beautiful ... until my mother saw them and told me they were *flor de muerto*, the flowers of the dead, the common Cuban name for marigolds. The sky was cloudy most days, and the sidewalks, houses, and road all seemed to blend together in an endless chain of grays broken only by the bright palettes of the large, leafy trees.

I was so engrossed in my world that I did not notice when Ramon arrived with Enriqueta and her sister a few hours later. The excitement at the door brought me back to reality. Ramon had found work at a local hotel as a dishwasher, and they had made a visit to the local Catholic school, where (by the grace of God and with a little help from my great-aunts' employer) I was to be accepted as a student beginning the next day. My family would have it no other way than my attending a Catholic school. Even in our impoverished state, religion ruled our lives.

Micaela looked at me fondly and told me I would like the school, and she made an effort to reassure me that everything would be well. It was, in fact, much too early to start school; I still needed rest from the long journey from Cuba and was too tired to start the next day. Nonetheless, it was done, and the river of our new life carried me like a small, rudderless boat along fast-moving currents that emptied into an unknown sea.

I had always loved school. It was my refuge and the bright spot in my day, but that was back in Cuba. Lately, however, things had become difficult, and school had become less about learning and more about political indoctrination. There were no more songs and stories and childlike drawings filled with bright colors. We had lined up in the courtyard every morning, and the familiar anthem and welcome song were replaced with harsher, more militant tunes. We were routinely drilled to gather if we had seen or heard any antigovernment chatter or activity in our home. If we had, we were instructed to immediately share this information with our teachers. Our spectrum of color had been reduced to olive green, the signature hue of the soldiers' uniforms. The now-familiar combination of red and black, the colors of the revolution, had replaced the red, white, and blue of our beloved Cuban flag. I wondered what I would do and what I would say in this new Santa Maria School. Everyone spoke in English. Frightened at the prospect and not ready to face the new reality that had crept so quickly into my young life, I prayed many Hail Marys that night and asked the kind lady in the blue robes to help me in her school so I could learn everything about this strange new place called Stamford.

Later that evening, I heard Herminia speaking on the phone with a friend of hers. It was a surprise because Mother never had many friends, but I knew Marina. She and Herminia had been friends since they were ten years old, and they had reconnected with each other after our move to La Habana. In a telephone call that was rare, brief, and expensive, she told Marina of the journey to Stamford and said we were slowly adjusting to our new surroundings. Nothing more could be said, as the lines were most likely tapped. We would soon find out that Marina and her family's departure from the island was imminent.

I had rarely seen my parents argue, but there was one time while we were in Cuba. Marina was visiting, and they had a serious disagreement. I had caught another of my frequent colds, and Abuela had made some traditional concoction for me to take, but I didn't seem to get better. I cried and fussed all night, and on the second day, when things continued without improvement, Ramon and Abuela had a heated discussion after he uncharacteristically raised his voice and told me to go to sleep, accusing Tomasa of island quackery and backward ways. Herminia entered the room, and in a chillingly calm, monotone voice, she told him to leave me alone and to show her mother respect. The house was silent, and the implied threat hung in the air for days. Marina and her middle son, who were our guests, felt sorry for me because I was small and sick and, in their opinion, not being given the correct medical treatment. They never forgot the incident, and we remembered it together many years later, when the young man became my husband and Marina my cherished mother-in-law.

Herminia woke me up the next morning, and suddenly I remembered that I was going to school. She had told me the day before that Abuela and Abuelo were coming to live with us in two months. I had jumped for joy and said a little prayer for them to arrive safely. Rarely did I see my mother smile, but she did as surely as the sun rose that morning, when she walked over and told me she had something important to share with me. Hearing of the impending arrival of my Abuela and Abuelo filled me with such a warm sensation of love and joy that I could feel my chest rise and fall with emotion. I had a skewed sense of time at that moment and felt as though I would see them the next day. The news began to erase the deep and aching sense of longing I felt for them both. They were the missing pieces, and now the little puzzle that had become my life would be complete. I checked the tears that collected behind my eyes, not wanting to mar the moment with any hint of sadness.

Ramon had gone to work that morning. He had more than one job, but his main one was factory work, as a machinist, where he worked long, hard hours to provide for our family.

As we stepped out into the sunny but cool early fall day, Herminia again repeated what had become her mantra: that the sun here was in the sky to make it pretty. She complained that it was like a lightbulb that was useless and *fundido*, burned out. The registration process for me to enter school had been prearranged and completed, and Herminia had visited the school with my father the day before and knew where to go. She said nothing as we walked into the building via the side door and headed for the classroom, which was on the right side of a green-tiled hallway.

I can still remember how the sounds of our footsteps echoed down the long corridor on that clear October morning. When we arrived at the door, Sister Mary Evangelist took my hand and led me through the cavernous classroom, where all eyes were upon me. Herminia's retreating footsteps were barely audible in the background, dim and fading, and I realized that she had left me here on what was to be my first day in an American classroom, alone.

Blurry shadows of faces could be seen through my tears, and my heart was as tight as the knot in my throat. I was gripped by a merciless fear as strange and unintelligible sounds could be heard around me. Morning prayers had begun at Saint Mary's School, but my only clues were the small hands of the students surrounding me making the familiar sign of the cross, as I did not speak one word of English. I had expressed concern to both of my parents about this fact, and although I know they empathized, as neither of them spoke any English upon arrival in the United States, they were confident in their little daughter's ability to pick it up quickly, and so they sent me off without so much as "good morning" in my repertoire.

For the terrified little girl standing motionless on the steps of this Tower of Babel, there was only one thing to do. I ran through the door and out into the now-deserted hallway to find that the familiar figure was long gone. I was led to my seat, and the realization was hard upon me for the first in what would be many times in my life that I was on my own.

For the rest of the day, the little boat adrift at sea was a curiosity for her fellow classmates. There were no other refugee children at the school, and certainly no one who did not speak English. I must say that most of the students were eager to be guides, helpers, and protectors of their new charge as the days went on. Like a dry sponge in a basin full of water, I absorbed every drop of newness around me. I was praised for new words and sentences, selected to visit the office as a buddy messenger, and invited to join the other girls at the lunch table in the cafeteria, where the hot lunches were a culinary adventure each and every day. The sisters were kind and nurturing to me, and I later realized that to them I was a symbol of the struggle against Communism that was headline news at the time.

Shortly after my arrival at the school, we were taken out of the classroom each day to practice a special exercise in the long, gleaming hallway. Each student would sit with his or her back to one of the green lockers and lower his or her head while wrapping his or her arms around his or her knees. We did this daily, until it became automatic. I would later learn that this was in preparation for an attack believed to be imminent during the Cuban Missile Crisis. Some of the students cried, but I simply did as I was told. I always closed my eyes during the time we were in practice and felt a familiar fear. For you see, I was no stranger to drills. While in Cuba, we prepared nightly for attack from America by stripping mattresses and leaning them against the wall, where we sandwiched ourselves while the air raid sirens wailed in the night air outside our balcony.

My love of school returned with a passion, and I worked hard every evening to master reading in the language of my new country, to the sheer delight of Ramon, who would eagerly listen to my efforts for a few minutes each evening as he prepared to go from his day job to one of the ones he held at night. This focus on learning would be his lasting legacy to me. He put it above all else and ensured I was given unlimited time for schoolwork. Once Abuelo and Abuela eventually arrived to live with us, this became a theme of battle between Abuela and Ramon. She insisted that I needed to learn the basics of homemaking, which was the ultimate goal of any self-respecting Cuban girl, while he insisted that I needed to nurture my God-given intellect. The taut rope in this familiar tug-of-war, I stretched myself thin to try to please them both. Time, and my increasing academic success, eventually loosened Abuela's grip and allowed Ramon to emerge victorious.

My assimilation started when I entered school. I began to speak English, watch American television (I loved TV, especially shows like *Gidget*), and enjoy American foods (like pizza and hot dogs and hamburgers). I was beginning to adjust to the American life, which was quite interesting and different from anything I'd ever experienced.

One Saturday morning, I woke up to hear some noises coming from the living room. Apparently Herminia had fainted when she had gotten out of bed that morning. I had always known her to be very fragile and sick, but I never knew the reason or extent. Ramon had his head buried in his hands, and I was scared to think she would die. Abuela was sitting by Herminia's side, holding her hand and stroking her hair, telling her that she would be all right and that it was for the best. I found out years later that my mother was prone to miscarriages. Tomasa blamed Ramon and added these events to the many beads of hatred for him that hung around her neck like an unholy rosary.

In the years that followed, Herminia's health affected us in many ways. She was always frail and needed attention and care. She did not become an independent person, never drove or managed the house or the finances. She suffered from many maladies, like migraines, anemia, and cancer, and she had multiple surgeries as well. She did manage to work but was often sick on the job. Therefore, Ramon often helped her, as they worked at the same factory. He would complete his piecework at a maniacal pace so he could run over to her station and ensure that she would meet her quota. I was an only child for twelve years, until the change-of-life arrival of my sister. In later years,

I realized that there would have been a sibling older than me, one younger, and then sibling twins. Had they all lived, we would have been a family of six children.

In Cuba, Herminia worked for a brief time at a dry cleaner's, but poor health did not let her work much outside the home. When she came to the United States, she did some hotel cleaning and then factory work. Abuela and Abuelo had to come live with us not only because it was the expected, customary thing to do in our culture but also so they could take care of me in light of my mother's poor health and Ramon's busy work schedule. Due to Mother's health and Father's busy schedule, Tomasa ran the house. She did all the cooking, cleaning, and at times, decision making. My abuelo was a military man. He was a colonel, and he played the clarinet in the army band. He was neat, quiet, and very intelligent. He read voraciously and knew a lot about many topics. When he arrived here, he took menial jobs washing dishes in a hotel restaurant to help the family. He liked to read and smoke, and he shared his knowledge and wisdom with many of the younger people in the family. He and my father tentatively got along, but he often told Ramon that he needed to develop more patience and that when he was older and more mature, he would understand the need for it.

Marina came to visit with her daughter, Elisa. Marina was a lovely woman who looked young for her age. The visit was very much like it would have been had we still been in Cuba. My family kept all our Cuban ways in this new land. We ate Cuban food, spoke Spanish, read Spanish newspapers, and watched Channels 41 and 47, the only Spanish-speaking stations available at the time. Once our door was closed, we were a Cuban family. While the old friends talked, Elisa and I played with my dolls and Abuela was, as always, busy in the kitchen, preparing a delicious typical Cuban meal of rice, beans, seasoned meat, and fried plantains. We felt so at home with them, and after the meal, we could see that the adults had visibly relaxed and were laughing and telling stories about the old days. They were feeling almost normal again—meaning that the specter of exile had left them for a bit and they were able to revel in the ways of their now-vanished homeland. They were back on the island, at least for a little while, and I closed my eyes and went there, too.

Chapter 5

New England Celebrations

October 1961 brought with it the first chill of a New England fall. Walking to school in one of the lacy pastel summer dresses hand-made by Tomasa, with only short white socks, I could feel the brisk morning air grow colder by the minute. I still wore the only jacket I owned, the one I had brought with me from Cuba. It was a bolero type made from a dusty rose colored wooly material and lined in pink satin, making it that much colder. Instead of buttons, it had two pieces of yarn hanging from the collar, with a rose pink pom-pom attached to the end of each. These were tied in a bow and allowed every degree of cold wind to enter. The back was heavily embroidered in a Mexican motif, with guitars, cacti, and ponchos. One particular morning, I cried from the cold, and my mother took notice. Something must have been said and done to this effect because the next day I woke to find a little plaid coat with a zipper and a hood on the back of a kitchen chair. It fit, and I wore it faithfully. It came, as did most of our clothes in those first few months, from a rummage store near the center of town, popular with the few newly arrived Cuban families. Ramon was a proud man, and he loathed the idea of his only daughter wearing secondhand clothing. That Christmas, he took me to a nice department store in town and spent what I now realize was almost a week's pay to purchase a beautiful red velvet coat with white fur trim on the border and hood, and fancy Tyrolean-like embroidery around the edges. Warm and beautiful, that coat forever symbolized his hard work and the start of his American Dream for our family.

Halloween was fast approaching, and everyone at school was excited about their new costumes. I had no clue about this upcoming holiday, as we never celebrated it back on the island. My cousin Luis came over to our house every day. He was my mother's first cousin's second son and the brother I never had. As an only child, I relished his visits because they afforded me the only opportunity to play with another child my age, as I was never allowed to go outside and mingle with the neighborhood children until I was very much older, due to my family's fear of this unfamiliar country's permissive ways. I wanted to be allowed to play outside, which my grandmother would not easily allow me to do, and ride my bike through the neighborhood. I also wanted to attend slumber parties, which were forbidden. I had asked Ramon about participating in the Halloween tradition, and much to Abuela and Herminia's protestations, he agreed to allow us to go to the neighboring homes for treats. Luis and I were nervous but excited, and that late afternoon, we donned our masks (purchased at Woolworth's for about ten cents), took two paper grocery bags with the edges rolled down a bit, and headed out to our first house.

The lights on the porch were on, and we rang the bell and waited. Luis wore a devil mask, and I wore a princess mask, the kind with the rubber elastic that went around the back of your head and had cut-out eyes, and slits for the nose and mouth. An older couple opened the door and peered at us. We stared right back. The lady was kind and said hello, and asked if we wanted to ask for something. Realizing that we were not your typical "trick-or-treaters," she smiled and told us what to say, rehearsing it with us until we repeated it with her. Then she gave us several pieces of candy and a few bars of what we recognized as chocolate. We smiled and ran down the porch steps, ready for the next house, carrying our currency for candy in that little phrase: "trik-o-tree."

November brought another unknown holiday, and I explained it to Ramon and Herminia one evening after we studied it in school. It seems that some of the other members of the community had already been discussing it, especially since it was to be a day off with family, a rare occasion to be sure. Preparations were made in the kitchen, and the day before the feast, I saw what looked to be an unusually large chicken, fragrant with garlic and onions, covered and placed in the refrigerator. We celebrated that first Thanksgiving with family and ate our first turkey, but with a Cuban flair. Rice and beans replaced asparagus and mashed potatoes, and pumpkin flan was our apple pie. No one in Stamford was more fervent in their giving thanks that year than the motley group of exiles in that little apartment on Lockwood Avenue.

During the summer holiday, a friend from school had a slumber party and I begged Ramon to allow me go there, but initially he refused. After much persuasion, he finally agreed. I arrived at the party, and there were lots of children from my class. I was really excited. Ramon had reluctantly left, and I went to join them. We had lots of fun. It was a beach house, and my friend's parents started a fire for us to sit around. We took turns in telling stories, played games, ate marshmallows, and sang songs. It was a really fun day. At ten at night, my friend's nanny came to where we sat and said my father was at the door asking to take me home. I was really sad and embarrassed because the fun had just begun. I meekly stood up, said my goodbyes, and headed inside to pack my stuff. I met father, who was standing by the door. I grumbled a greeting, and he helped me with my bag. He thanked my friend's parents, who by now had been alerted to the situation, and we left. The car ride home was silent and uncomfortable, as a few hot, angry tears of frustration rolled down my cheeks. When I got home, my mother was sick with a migraine again, and I sat beside her for familiarity, not expecting consolation because what had happened was the norm and she was probably sick because of my father's decision to let me go to the event in the first place. I eventually fell asleep, and Ramon must have carried me to bed, because when I woke up to pee, I found myself in my room. That one incident clearly showed me where the line in the sand was drawn by my family, separating me all my growing years from my American friends. I struggled daily as I swam in the turbulent waters of the channel between my two lives. Perhaps the illusion of returning to Cuba made my parents protective of allowing me to become "too" American. But as I grew older, I realized this was my new home, and I dove deeper and deeper into the waters of my assimilation, all the while holding on to the life-preserver of my Cuban culture and identity.

I was a student at Saint Mary's in 1963 when there seemed to be something heavy hanging in the air. The sisters murmured to one another, and some of them were visibly distraught and crying. I sat still and waited for information, the old, familiar fear rising up just enough to cause my breathing to speed up. We were told to stand, get our things, and line up in the familiar two rows in the hallway. We were walked over the few steps to the massive, cathedral-like church in silence. The pews were already filling up with the older students, and as we waited for our seats, a couple of the older girls were overheard saying: "The statues are crying. Their eyes are crying blood!" I froze in place, reminded of Abuela's beliefs and stories, and slowly I entered the pew and knelt down as instructed. Immediately the booming voice of the monsignor told us the news: "President Kennedy has been shot. We will now pray for him together." After a string of Our Fathers, Hail Marys, and Glory Bes, we were dismissed, row by row, and told to go right home. At that time, the majority of the students walked to and from school, and there was still the small-town feeling of safety for children on the sidewalks. By this time, I was visibly grieved by the news that the US president, whose handsome, smiling photo hung in my classroom, was fighting for his life. I entered the small apartment, to the surprise of my abuela, who immediately peppered me with questions as I made my way to the television set. There it was, in black and white, the convertible, the voiceover, and the reality that the president was dead. My grandmother stared at me, stone-faced, as I struggled to tell her the news.

She roughly grabbed my shoulders and said, "Do not shed one tear for that man, do you hear me, not one tear!" I stood still as she said almost maniacally, "The walls of hell are at this moment being decorated with his head! ... All of those poor young boys died en la Bahia de Cochinos, the Bay of Pigs, because he broke his word to them ... The devil take him!"

I sat for a long time and stared at the television, so sad and so confused. The man revered at school by the sisters was reviled at home by my Abuela. That evening, I overheard the conversations of my parents and grandparents, along with the many telephone conversations with other Cubans in the community, and overwhelmingly, although they fiercely loved this country, because of that one incident, they did not share the grief that enveloped America on that gray November day. It was many years later that I would begin to pull back the curtain on that event, to reveal a historical moment when a band of trained Cuban militants would attempt to reclaim their homeland, believing they would be supported in their effort by the American president. When the moment arrived, that help was not in sight. When the president had consulted his brother, Robert, he counseled him against any involvement in the plan, and the absence of the American military resulted in the young men being slaughtered on the beach in their attempt to overtake the island. This failed invasion helped me to understand how a group of exiles who had such deep love and gratitude for this country could react so violently to a president's death. Their anger, fueled by the loss of the young lives trying to regain their island home, temporarily blinded them to this national tragedy.

My mother's sickness was getting worse by the day. She had to undergo a surgery that could only be done in New York. Father had to take time off of work to go with her. Abuela and Abuelo stayed with me at home. They came back after a few days with the news that mother was pregnant. I didn't know whether to be happy or sad because I had had my hopes up in the past that I was going to have a little brother or sister. I just took the news as it came. To my surprise, nine months went by, and she gave birth to a baby. I was twelve years old at the time. During the course of mother's pregnancy, there were times when I thought she was going to lose the baby. Mother was forty years old and was told by the doctors that it was a high-risk pregnancy and she had to be well taken care of. Any little mismanagement could lead to a miscarriage. Father tried his best but had to work as much as ever. One evening, Mother had just eaten and wanted to relax for a bit. She was walking back into her room when she slipped and fell. I was alarmed and screamed out to Abuela and Abuelo. There was blood all over. Father was out, and I didn't know what to do. Abuela then quickly told me to dial for an ambulance, and once I did, it came within a few minutes. Herminia was rushed to the hospital, where the doctor examined her and said there was a possibility that she had lost the baby. He said it was a hemorrhage and asked that we wait till the bleeding stopped. A few hours later, he came in to check on my mother and did a test. He told us that the baby was all right. He said he was really surprised and that mother had been strong through the ordeal, something we were all surprised to hear at the time but that I confirmed in later years as time wore on. He asked that she be careful next time to avoid slipping. Father came in as soon as he heard and calmed down when he heard she was out of danger. She was discharged on the fourth day. When we got home, everyone, including me, was always looking out for Herminia and gave her a helping hand with anything she wanted to do, including walking.

On the due date, I had just come from school, and Abuela was making dinner. I went in to see Mother and saw that she was asleep. I went to take a bath and change into clean clothes. I joined Abuela in the kitchen, and we talked. Abuela said that Herminia was to be taken to the hospital that day for a *caesaria*. She did not explain, and I later researched the term in my *World Book Encyclopedia*. I taught myself the meaning, as I had done with many words countless times before and continued to do throughout my growing-up years. We stayed home and did not accompany my father and mother to the hospital. Abuela prepared a Cuban specialty believed to be specifically nourishing for new mothers. We were all happy with the new addition to the family born that Memorial Day 1965. Herminia left the hospital ten days later, and we began the adjustment to having a baby in a house full of adults and one almost teenager. Herminia went back to work as soon as allowed, and Tomasa fully assumed the responsibility for child care and rearing, as she had done when I was born. Being twelve years older than my sister was at times fun because I was sometimes allowed to take care of her like a mother. I liked to help bathe her and dress her up when I came home from school, which my father usually frowned upon. He would say that after school was homework time and that it was my grandmother's job to take care of the baby. I would dutifully listen, although I would routinely check on her and oftentimes read her a story. I loved my sister but admit that having a sibling later in life was at times a mixed blessing.

Father didn't spend much time with us, as he was always working, I though he worked a little too hard, but it was all to make a better life for us. When my sister was still small, Mother and Father decided to throw her a little party. I had many birthday parties when I was a child, but it had been different back then, when we were on the island. Fancy dresses, outdoor games, and the requisite piñata on the balcony, as well as the familiar tastes from local establishments, were the order of the day, as was the rich, sweet cake from La Gran Via bakery, known for its masterpieces. For my sister's birthday, there was a cake, a few simple decorations, and lots of delicious Cuban food. Along with the usual group of family and friends who always gathered at holidays and all special occasions, a few guests from my mother and father's workplace were invited. There were gifts, many handmade, laughter, and camaraderie. I will always remember those times of close-knit family events, and the feeling of togetherness unmatched by any other. We had little in those days, but we had a lot. Looking back, even after everyone grew older and more accomplished, no amount of success or material acquisition could hold a candle to the joy, warmth, and authenticity of those simple gatherings. I play some of them over in my mind, like vintage films, and watch the faces and smiles of those now long departed fade softly, like still frames in an aging reel.

Chapter 6

Translations

At school, I enjoyed each passing day because my English had improved by leaps and bounds; three months into the school year, I was able to have conversations in correct English, with no trace of an accent. Unlike my parents, who had so much on their plates and little time to learn the language, I now enjoyed having conversations at school without the teacher addressing me specifically to make sure I understood what was being taught in class.

Through the first few months of my learning English, I did not suffer the same pangs of fear and embarrassment that older people do when speaking a new language. My attempts were made with no hesitancy and with a carefree abandon unavailable to adults, since I was eight years old, after all.

I remember one particular evening when Ramon got back from work, lamenting how difficult it was to learn this new language. I felt sorry for him because initially I had felt left out at school due to my inability to speak English, despite the good efforts of my classmates to include me. His type of work did not require a lot of talking, since it consisted of washing dishes and cleaning floors. He said that when he made a mistake or used the wrong word while trying to explain something to a supervisor, the other workers laughed at him instead of helping him.

Abuela was of the opinion that he ought to confront them for their mockery and that this would shut them up for good. That was Abuela for you. Just let your fists do the talking, and you would find no language barrier there! He responded that her advice would not work and would result in the loss of his job, which we all knew was precious. He said he had a plan to bring his coworkers around in a more logical way. Abuela was convinced that his tormentors would not see him differently unless he took action, but he disagreed. Despite his at times fiery exterior temperament, Ramon was, in his heart, a man of God. My father and I started having conversations in English at home, and sometimes on the few occasions when he was back from work early enough for me to see him, I would cajole him to assist with my homework. Those were happy, rare bonding moments for my father and me, and I look back fondly on my family's insistence that, despite our believed-to-be temporary stay in this country, I learn the language thoroughly. Soon my newfound linguistic talents were in high demand in the small, tight-knit Cuban community that had established itself in Stamford, and Ramon took enormous pride in announcing that his daughter would serve as translator for any occasion necessary. This "translator" job brought me a lot of exposure, bringing with it many unfamiliar offices and a great variety of people, some kind and some cruel.

A few of the front-line secretaries who protected the inner sanctums of doctors and lawyers were amused by the presence of this tiny girl who was the spokesperson for their client or patient. The majority was not as accommodating and saw me as little more than a trained parrot and a nuisance. In one such occasion, a particularly sour clerical sneered and told me that I would not be allowed to enter the consultation room. She would not be moved, and my father and his friend went in without me. Less than a minute later, the ruddy-faced physician poked his head into the waiting room, signaled for me to come in, and shook his head at the secretary. As I walked past the clerk, I glanced at her and demurely smiled. Abuela had taught me well. The doctor had quickly realized that neither of the men spoke English and that I was there for a good reason.

I credit these assignments with giving me my growing assertiveness and confidence in my English-speaking abilities.

Herminia was not as eager to learn English as the rest of us. I could credit this to her minimal interactions with people. For the first few months we were in America, she was indoors, dreading all contact with the outside world until there was a dire need for another source of income beside Ramon's. Sometimes I wondered why Abuelo and Abuela sheltered her so much. I had two answers: being the only child and being sickly. She had many acquaintances but few close friends, and her loneliness would have been worse had she not married such a devoted man.

A few months later, Ramon was getting better at his English, and I even got him to start writing simple sentences in one of my old notebooks. He was reluctant at first to write. He felt he was just fine with speaking English. Little did he know how this step would benefit him in the future and make his earlier dream, of serving God through the Church as an ordained deacon, reality.

Teaching my father and a few people from Stamford the basics of English made me feel responsible for everyone and urged me to continue to work hard in school. It also, unbeknownst to me at the time, prepared me in earnest for my future profession in the field of education.

This new life was in a transitional stage for all of us, and we were grateful for the opportunity to have left the island and to have been reunited with my grandparents. We were all a little worse for the wear, but we were moving forward. You see, our family was one that appreciated the little things while expecting the big ones. We had conversations in English at times, but Spanish was still used in our home as the main language. The family preferred me to speak in Spanish rather than in English, and I understood their position, although I did not fully embrace it.

Weekends were the only time we had true family time, as Ramon worked multiple jobs and Herminia had taken up housekeeping jobs at nearby motels. Abuelo worked his restaurant job, and Abuela ran the house like a majordomo. The coming years were comprised mostly of studying, and school was my main activity. I also held a small part-time job in retail and babysat for neighbors on occasion (my father despised both of these latter activities, since he only wanted me to study and get good grades). He once spoke to me privately about my taking on these jobs. He said I would not be able to focus on my studies, and I would be distracted. I told him not to worry—that although these jobs made me feel responsible and independent, I understood what my priority needed to be. I think on that day he was overcome with worry for my future, sadness for what was no more, and the realization that his little daughter was growing up, because until that day, I had never seen my father shed a tear.

It was less than a year since we had arrived in America, and my reports were showing good progress. Ramon was happy with the outcome. Although he was pleased, he pointed out that a ninety-eight was not one hundred and that he knew I could do a bit better. He explained that all the sacrifices he had made in the past year and the dangers we faced leaving Cuba were all in the name of the future of his child, and he could not imagine a life of such hardship and grueling work for me in the years ahead. Remembering that moment, I saw clearly through what I had then perceived to be his perfectionism and saw the pure love of a father for his daughter.

A few years later, Ramon bought a Chevrolet station wagon. He bought this particular car because he was a huge fan of *Bonanza* and he watched the same advertisements every Sunday, depicting the All-American family "seeing the USA in their Chevrolet."

The car did not initially live up to its expectations, and it saw more of the shop than the road. Because there was no lemon law at the time, Ramon asked me to contact the dealer, who referred me to the home office. Way before the age of computers and the Internet, I called the number and was given an address to which to send our complaint in writing. I crafted a letter under Ramon's watchful direction, making sure to include all the details and his description of what he deemed had been false advertising.

Many weeks passed, and Ramon received a call from the dealership. He was astonished when they asked him to bring in the car, and they replaced it with a new one. Over the years, I saw many instances where he would demand quality or fair treatment. Unlike Herminia, who would stay in the car or walk away from the scene in sheer mortification, I would stand in place and absorb every exchange like an eager pupil. The education I received at my father's side rivaled my academic one, and what I learned was just as useful, if not more so. He was my teacher, and school was in session.

My grandparents lived with us their entire lives. They never left my mother (their only child), as this was common practice in the Cuban community. Both of my grandparents were cared for in our home until their deaths.

My grandfather died at sixty-five years of age from a heart attack. I was home with my grandmother, and I always went in to say goodnight to him before turning in. A while later, my grandmother woke me up and asked me to call my parents at the factory (they worked the night shift), and then I called the fire department to send an ambulance to our home. He was dead on arrival. My grandmother outlived him by many years, and she also had a heart attack at the age of eighty-six while sitting in her favorite blue chair, which faced both the TV and the door, so she could monitor the comings and goings of the family. They were both solidly important figures in my life.

My mother did not work much and was extremely dependent on my father, and her parents before him. She had been sickly for most of her life and had endured thyroid cancer and a long and difficult surgery.

In my mind, I remember her suffering from migraines and in a darkened room many days because of her photophobia. My father was my role model and the person who most molded me throughout my life. I loved both of my parents, but my father was the one I resembled most in every way and from whom many of my personality traits stemmed.

My little sister was a charming firecracker of a girl. I looked out for her as much as I could, as she was mostly cared for by Abuela. I served as a link to the outside American world. Obviously more American than I was, she was very intelligent and started school quite early. She was enrolled in a local Catholic school but was not a big fan of classrooms, teachers, and rules. She had many friends, and Ramon allowed her go out to slumber parties and didn't show up at the doorstep of the hosts like he did during my time. Both Ramon and Herminia had mellowed significantly with age, and as a result, my sister enjoyed a permissiveness in her growing years that was foreign to me. I had not been given any of the liberties she was granted. After Abuelo died, I was left with increasing responsibilities in taking care of my sister. To me, she never really grew up, and I still see her as that little girl I remember—pretty, naughty, and very headstrong. As my mother and father still had to work hard, I was put in the position of assisting with her care and the expectation was that I would help my grandmother to do so. I drove a car, so I would pick her up from school as needed. I must admit, as a teenager, it cramped my style a bit to have to worry about how this would interfere with my many activities at school and my social life. But ever the dutiful daughter, I always did as I was told. There is a photo of us in my high school yearbook that always served as a testament to those days. I missed the photo op with my friends for the "informal" shot, and when I arrived with my sister, flushed and hurried from a school pickup, the photographer asked us both to pose, and we did. The photo served as a lifelong reminder of duty to family.

Growing up in America taught me that different stories define us and that the people who make up this vast country and hailed from diverse ethnic backgrounds had varying experiences coming here. Hard work and economic survival, keeping family traditions, valuing education, and holding religious beliefs are only a few of the threads that make up the fabric of the immigrant tapestry.

Chapter 7

New Beginnings

The days passed and somehow turned into years. Life became routine for us all. Ramon, Herminia, and Abuelo worked, Abuela kept the house, cooking and cleaning to perfection, and I went to school every day filled with dreams of becoming a translator at the United Nations. I was inspired by one of the translators who came to give a speech at a UN ceremony at my school. She was applauded when announced to take the stage, looking beautiful, well dressed, and visibly respected as a man held her hand for support as she climbed up to the stage. She spoke so fluently, and everyone listened with rapt attention. As I sat there looking at her, I was lost in my own world imagining myself up there, speaking all those grammatically correct phrases and having people respect me as they did her. As soon as the ceremony ended, I waited behind to see if I could speak with her, but she seemed busy talking with the administrators in attendance and the sisters. As soon as I saw her approaching as she prepared to leave, I quickly walked toward her before she could be hijacked by another eager fan. When I introduced myself, she was polite and answered all my questions. Her name was Amanda, and I remember thinking it was the most beautiful name I had ever heard. I asked her how she had become a translator. She responded that she went to a university to study languages and said she was working to earn her doctorate. Because I looked perplexed, she explained what that was in simple terms. She advised that I read lots of books because they were the best teachers. She apologized for not being able to speak with me for too long, and as she turned to leave and wave, I was the essence of an impressionable girl who had just been touched by an angel of hope and possibility.

Although my circle had expanded to include some of my American friends from school and the neighborhood, we were still a tightly knit, unassimilated group of immigrants at heart, with most of the adults simply biding their time until we returned to our island home. There was always a sense of deep gratitude for America but no sense of permanence. Realization set in slowly and was most palpable at the funerals of the older members of the community, who began to die in exile. As a little girl surrounded by Cubans on one side and Americans on the other, I worked hard to straddle these widely different worlds, almost to the point of breaking. At times, especially during the Missile Crisis, I felt like the odd man out, because although in my home we sided unconditionally with the United States, I was still a Cuban national with a green card and not yet "officially" American. We watched newscasts and programs on Canal 41 or 47, read *El Diario La Prensa* for our newspaper, and listened to ballads old and new on Radio WADO. I really loved to watch the mainstream programs in English that were so popular on the television in the 1960s, as they were the unlatched gate to the process of my assimilation into the American world. But each time I switched on the magical box, Ramon's words would always echo in my ear: "Have you finished your homework and read your books?" Weekends were spent mostly reading, when we were not at Mass or on the occasional outing if Ramon had a rare day of freedom from work.

We bought our first home, a brick-façade condo in a residential section of our still, small town. I remember we moved to our new house a day before my birthday, and I was really excited to be celebrating it there. My little sister was also excited about the move, and the night before, we had begun to select which of our things to pack into the small boxes we were given and place those in a corner near where other boxes had already been placed. We could barely close our eyes to sleep. Very early the next morning, my sister woke me up, and we both jumped out of bed to see that the movers had already arrived. They consisted of an assortment of friends and family members who had come to help my father, who in turn had, or would, help them. Abuela had gone to the new house to clean it, in the way only she could do. She had already previously fully cleaned the old house, as was her custom. Aside from making sure the new tenants would not think us unclean, she wanted to ensure that our new abode was cleaned to her standards. I also knew well by then that cleaning held otherworldly significance for her, in keeping with her Santeria beliefs. The house was not too big, but I thought it was perfect! Ramon lovingly painted the patio and planted flowers for Herminia and was an enviable handyman who kept the place pristine. He tended to the flowers every day and made sure the grass was well groomed at all times. We had three levels, and the finished cellar level became the hub for gatherings for family and friends on many holidays and special occasions. I vividly remember summers during those years because Ramon had the largest American flag on the block proudly displayed by early morning. Every year, a small-town parade would roll down the main road, to the delight of everyone who put chairs out on the sidewalk. Our little family would sit there, proud as peacocks, savoring this tiny slice of the American Dream.

My sister Terri, as she liked to be called, was growing up, and her experience was unique. At home she was a little stranger in a strange land, surrounded by a family who had come from a place she had never seen, spoke a language she did not completely understand, and embraced foods and customs very different from those of her neighborhood friends. I often think how bizarre it must have been for her to have her whole world tinged with vestiges of a place she had always heard about but never visited. Perhaps this explained her rebellious resistance to all things Cuban and her emphatic assertions that she was nothing if not American.

Those happy years were intertwined with moments of deep sadness, as we lost friends and family members, and Herminia saw early retirement when she suffered a heart attack at work. It happened on a Wednesday afternoon when Herminia had been working for two straight shifts, which she didn't usually do. She had wanted to take the next day off, so she decided to work more than her usual hours. She was scheduled to clock out in the next hour, when she suddenly felt a strong grip on her chest. It subsided, and she thought it was over until few seconds later when she again clutched her chest in pain. She was immediately rushed to the hospital, where the doctor was able to stabilize her. We were advised to have her go on bed rest for a few days before returning to work. We all thought that after a few days off, she would return to work, not knowing that she and Ramon had already decided that she was finished with her many years of factory work.

I entered high school and dove even deeper into the world of academia and my studies. No longer that little outsider, timid and fearful of this new land, I was happy and confident as my new country now felt as familiar and comfortable to me as a well-worn, much-loved pair of favorite tennis shoes. I was very active in school activities and was near the top of my class academically.

My mother's health improved a bit after she stopped working, and this relieved everyone. It seemed that my little sister grew up very fast, and now she also attended Catholic school. She was precocious, articulate, and unlike me, very headstrong, as she often locked horns with the teachers and authority figures in charge. The teachers called the house on occasion and would ask me to relay to my father that they needed his help in their efforts to correct her. Abuela was getting old and sick, and I feared she might die soon. I didn't want to lose her just yet, as she still was a central figure in our family.

Years later, Micaela, who had already been in a convalescent home for a time due to her growing inability to live on her own, passed away. I remember her to this day as a fiercely independent member of the family, with an uncompromising outer shell, but with a unique, free air of excitement surrounding her and a soft, loving interior. Her death came as a sharp blow to me, despite her advanced age, and I miss her to this day. Ever the rebel, she left directives to not only be cremated but have her ashes scattered over her beloved Long Island Sound. This news shocked our staid, traditional family members, but I smiled inwardly at her ability to be true to herself, in death and beyond.

Chapter 8

Growing Older

One of the most important things in a Cuban girl's life was marriage and the family that inevitably would come with it. For all my American ways, in my house, I was no exception. While Ramon dreamed of college and caps and gowns and ceremonies, Herminia and Abuela, in no uncertain terms, had other expectations. This was comical to me because I was not allowed to simply date, like most other girls I knew. So it happened that I began to spend time with Marina's middle son, who had moved to our town the previous year. We went out to movies and bowling, with his sister and my cousin, as unchaperoned outings were out of the question.

It was around this time that I was became the proud recipient of a full scholarship to college offered by the factory where Ramon and Herminia worked to the employee son or daughter who demonstrated the highest academic excellence. Ramon was overwhelmed with pride, but it was not enough for him to simply let me skip happily off to the college of my choice. I had initially wanted to go to an Ivy League school, like Amanda. I never forgot her and the kind advice she had imparted on that long-ago day. But Ramon didn't want me to go that far, so we selected a school close to home, and after many tears and cajoling (and a visit to the dean), I was allowed to board at the College of New Rochelle. During my college days, I worked hard, and after four years of study, I earned my bachelor of arts degree in comparative literature, with minors in Spanish and French.

I had continued in a relationship with the man who would eventually become my husband, and time brought love, and love brought marriage. Our wedding was a grand affair, held in a Catholic Church, with a wonderfully fun hotel reception following. We honeymooned in the Canary Islands and visited Tenerife, the birthplace of my mother's paternal grandparents. Life after marriage was so different, as we assumed the responsibilities of true adulthood.

We set up our little apartment, and the following year, we had our first son, Laurence. He was a healthy and happy baby who resembled his father. He was joined a couple of years later by his brother Fernando, who looked very much like his grandfather Ramon. Before my thirtieth birthday, came Adrian, who reminded us of his paternal grandfather, who sadly did not live to see these grandsons. The boys grew up happily under our watch, each with their own look and personality, but they all shared their love and curiosity for the place where their mother and father were born, an island ninety miles from the tip of Florida called Cuba. I taught them to speak Spanish and cooked and fed them our traditional foods, and they, too, grew up in the center of an extended family filled with grandparents, aunts, uncles, cousins, and friends. Another older family member had also gotten married in the United States, but to an American man. This was met with a lot of objection, at first, by the bride's family. The groom was a kind and gentle man, and once he became a part of our family, we all made him feel welcome. I wouldn't have even thought about doing this, as Ramon would not have supported it one bit. In my youth, knowing the type of family I came from, I always thought it better to do things according to our accepted code of conduct. But others in the family were not the kind who dwelled on the Cuban tradition and so did not enforce it so strictly in their own families. This, like everything else, changed for all of us with time and with the passing of the old guard.

My sons became quite adept at playing dominoes, starting out on their father's lap and shuffling the tiles and calling out, "Aguita!"—the term used when mixing the tiles before distributing—from the time they were babies. They did well in school and knew that college was the direction in which they were headed. Once they entered school, I returned as well, securing a master's in education and then a sixth year in administration. It was difficult but satisfying to enter the teaching profession. It segued nicely with my duties as a mother. As the children grew, I became an administrator. When I was named principal of one of the local elementary schools, Ramon was in the small audience during the board of education vote, along with my children and family, all seated in the front row. He proudly raised his hand in response to the superintendent's question to the board regarding how many were in favor of my nomination for the position. I will hold that moment in my heart for as long as I live.

I didn't let my sons grow up the way I did by not letting them mix with their peers, especially because they were American and because they were boys. But I did teach them many of our Cuban traditions, held them to our family expectations, and brought them up to be good men. This went a long way in shaping their lives, and I have always been so proud of them.

Chapter 9

Return and Redemption

It was a day unlike any other. The sun shone high in the sky like a beacon, guiding the hours that passed so slowly. Voices echoed through the house, and I caught the sound of my eldest son Larry's voice, rapidly and responsibly ticking off the list of things we needed for the trip. It mixed eerily with other voices in my head from long ago. Adrian, my youngest, stood smiling at the window, forecasting good flight weather for this time of the year. September, his birth month, is known for hurricanes, but none was expected in the next ten days. There was a knock at the door, and I hurriedly ran, opening it to the sight of my middle son, Fernando, tan and handsome, suitcase in hand. He was joining us on the journey. As we prepared to leave for Cuba together, the old, familiar voices of yesterday accompanied me on the journey.

My palms were sweaty, and I remembered my sons making the decision to visit Cuba at the end of the summer of 2016, when we had gathered for a family dinner. The topic was seldom brought up, but this time it seemed the boys had spoken among themselves and decided to broach the subject. At first I was adamant that I would not go. Too many years had passed, and too many memories were buried hard and deep. Best not to disturb the dead, Abuela always said. There was anger initially and then the deep sadness. My father's voice in my head said, "No vayas, mi hija" ("Don't go, my daughter"). After all, why should I be granted what was denied so many of them, those I knew and loved, who came here, worked hard, and never, ever got the chance to once more step on Cuban soil? But then the reality had hit me like a lightning bolt from Santa Barbara's hand (she who had been the source of my grandmother's strength): the homecoming was not for me; it was for them, for those that had left and never returned, for those who had never been, even though they carried the blood of the island in their veins. And here we were, tickets in hand, ready to make a return fifty-four years later. I had left as a little girl, my whole life a long, wide road stretching before me, unmarked and unknown. I was returning a mature woman, now racing to the finish line, hands filled with the experiences of a life well lived and a heart full of love and pride for the three sons who made my world complete. Once in the livery car, I looked out the window and saw the place I had called home for the bulk of my life pass by in a blur of neat homes and gardens, and trees that were starting to turn that now-familiar color of crimson, and I felt the slight chill that was the harbinger of the autumn to come. The check-in was fairly quick, and I was glad it was over. A seasoned traveler, this was no ordinary trip, and memories of long-ago fears brought a swarm of butterflies to my stomach. We boarded and sat together, three in a row and one across the aisle. The boys watched my face as the plane began its ascent. I tried hard to mask the great mix of emotion but was not successful. I was once again that little girl on the KLM flight so many years ago. No turning back now; life had taken me away, and now it was bringing me back, accompanied by my children. I was going home.

Weeks before, the boys and I had talked about going to Cuba. I was dead set against the idea, saying there was no need to take that trip … that there was nothing for me to go back to. In reality, I was scared to face the prospect of returning. I knew full well that going back to Cuba would bring a flood of memories, both sad and happy. Starting life as a child in Cuba had shaped me into the person I had become. The trip reminded me of Abuela and Abuelo—and of my parents, who were now gone. Surprisingly, Ramon died before Herminia. He succumbed suddenly to sepsis, and Herminia died of a heart attack many years later. Neither ever saw the island again.

Once in the air, we got comfortable in our seats, and I had this nostalgic feeling, remembering the time we left Cuba heading to Kingston, then to Miami, arriving in Stamford, and I sighed. I remembered Mr. Sahmuel's house, his never-ending stories, and those who had taken the trip with us, and I wondered where they all were today and what had become of them. Some would have definitely died along the way.

Having my sons close was the best thing that could have ever happened to me that day. I remembered when I was pregnant with my last child, Adrian. It was the most difficult pregnancy of the three. The doctor thought for sure I would have a miscarriage, but I was able to pull through. I had gone on bed rest until the due date. I couldn't do anything on my own and had to be assisted. Adrian was finally born, and I thought he was the most beautiful baby. He looked so small and helpless, but he was a very healthy baby. I cried as they put him in my arms, thinking he had almost not made the journey to this life, this world. I was so lost in thought that I didn't notice when we approached our destination. It was the pilot's announcement that jolted me back to reality. I peered out of the oval airplane window. The scenery coalesced into a portrait, evoking recollection. The colors conjured the past, and the Cuba of my memory came flooding back. I said a silent prayer of thanksgiving, smiled softly, and thought to myself, *Miriam, you have come back home at last.*

About the author

Miriam Isidro, a native of Cuba, settled in Stamford, Connecticut, after her exile from Cuba. She retired as an elementary school principal and is the mother of three sons born in the United States who appreciate their Cuban culture and history. She still lives in Stamford. This is her first book.

Miriam dressed to enjoy the Carnavales in Cuba.

Ramon, author's father, and her cherished mentor.

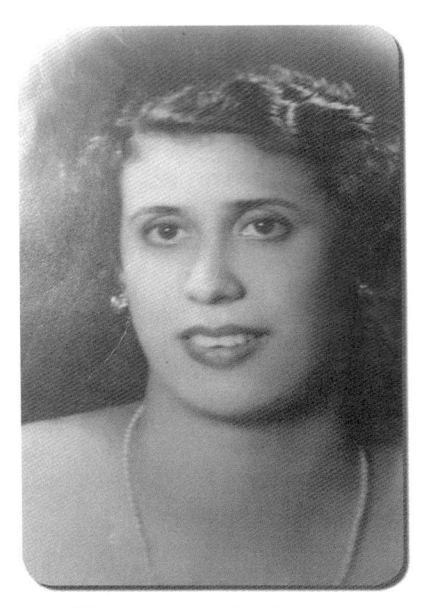

Herminia, author's mother, lovely and frail.

Tomasa, author's maternal grandmother, a Cuban beauty.

Alfonso, author's maternal grandfather in military uniform, a gentleman.

Miriam and her parents enjoying a horse-drawn carriage ride in Cuba

Author on her birthday,
with her parents in Cuba,
during happy times.

Miriam ready for school,
briefcase in hand, already
in love with learning.

Miriam in line to receive her 1st Communion in Cuba.

64

Author and her grandparents outside her home in Cuba, Calle Manglar.

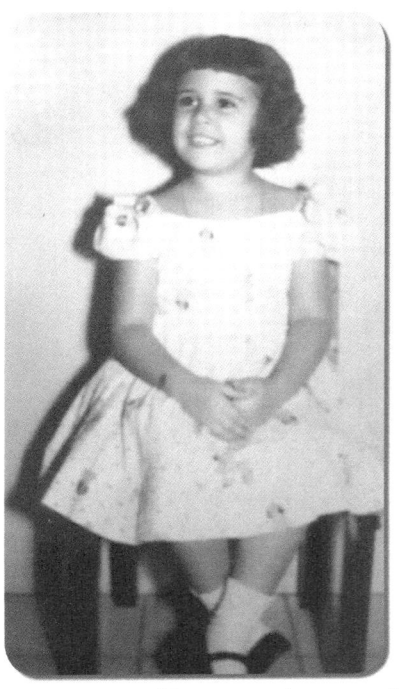

Miriam happy in one of her many homemade dresses.

Miriam's aunt and uncle on the steps of the rooming house in Jamaica.

Author with her parents on Easter Sunday on Suburban Avenue.

Miriam and family celebrating Thanksgiving, Cuban-style.

Ramon, at the first of many jobs held to provide for his family.

Author wearing the warm, red coat, a gift from her father.

Miriam in her school uniform surrounded by God and Country.

Author and family enjoying a rare outing in a nearby park.

Miriam's coming of age portrait at 15 years of age.

Author's beloved sons, Laurence, Adrian and Fernando.